Praise f(

Joretta Klepfer's newest publication, *JUST PRAY MORE!* is a blessing to people of all ages and in the varied stages of their walks in faith. As a Lutheran pastor, I am happy to have this additional resource to use with teenagers in confirmation classes. These scripture readings and heartfelt prayers serve as models of how our conversations with God are personal and yet universal. They capture our imagination and help us to remember the times in our lives when God has been revealed to us. *JUST PRAY MORE!* is a gift to all of us who might be reluctant to pull up a chair and talk to God. It is natural; it is about everyday events; it is genuinely authentic.

—The Reverend Mary Louise Sitton
St. Luke's Lutheran Church
Mount Ulla, North Carolina

Joretta Klepfer's new book will doubtless be appreciated by those who valued her first book of prayers, a fine and useful collection. This volume is centered on her love for Jesus, to whom she ascribes all godly functions, a "christocentric" theology. It is simple, sincere, lovely, and sometimes profound. She sees beyond and within things many people take for granted. Her writing is much like herself:

sunny and written with a passion for giving away what she loves so much.

—Grace Adolphsen Brame, Ph. D., is an author, lecturer, professional singer, and retreat leader; her most recent books are *Faith, the Yes of the Heart*, and *THE CROSS: PAYMENT OR GIFT? Rethinking the Death of Jesus*

JUST PRAY MORE!

JUST PRAY MORE!

more poetic prayers and prayerful poems

J O R E T T A   K .   K L E P F E R

TATE PUBLISHING
AND ENTERPRISES, LLC

Published by Tate Publishing & Enterprises, LLC
127 E. Trade Center Terrace | Mustang, Oklahoma 73064 USA
1.888.361.9473 | www.tatepublishing.com

Tate Publishing is committed to excellence in the publishing industry. The company reflects the philosophy established by the founders, based on Psalm 68:11,
"The Lord gave the word and great was the company of those who published it."

Book design copyright © 2015 by Tate Publishing, LLC. All rights reserved.
Cover design by Nikolai Purpura
Interior design by Jomel Pepito

Published in the United States of America

ISBN: 978-1-68028-282-5
Poetry / Subjects & Themes / Inspirational & Religious
15.01.09

Dedicated to the Glory of God
In honor of my family

Best Husband ever, Robert O. Klepfer, Jr. (Bob)

Best Son ever, Robert O. Klepfer, III (B3)

Best Mother ever, Margaret H. Kennerly

In memory of

Best Mother-in-law ever, Hilda M. Klepfer

Best Father-in-Law ever
Robert O. Klepfer-the original

Best Father ever, Mack G. Kennerly

Thank You

I am grateful…

for my family heritage of faith;

for the loving support of my husband, my son,
my mother, and all my family;

to Dr. Grace Brame,
Pastor John Chandler,
Pastor Mary Louise Sitton, and
Randy Youngquist-Thurow
for their generous comments of endorsement
for this book;

to the incredible team provided by Tate Publishing and
Enterprises, LLC.

This *thank you* is not truly sufficient but is offered
with much love and great joy.

Contents

Dear Readers,

The poems and prayers just keep coming—much the same as did the ones for my first book, *JUST PRAY! a book of poetic prayers and prayerful poems*. In the years since the submission of the first collection, they have just kept coming. Not so frequently perhaps, nor in quite the same style sometimes, but nevertheless they kept coming.

What an adventure!

It's time these poems/prayers have their own book, *JUST PRAY MORE! more poetic prayers and prayerful poems*. I have kept them in approximately the same order as they were written over the past several years.

Now it's your turn to be immersed in God's messages for us. Enjoy *JUST PRAY MORE! more poetic prayers and prayerful poems*.

May blessings of joy, peace, and love be yours.

Joretta Klepfer

Introduction

First, a bit of introduction to let me share
      my faith with you.
My grandfather's given name was Martin Luther.
      Need I say more about being a Lutheran?

It's my heritage and it's also my choice!

It's my choice because
      I love the music,
            I love the liturgy, but most of all,
                  I love the message!

Jesus, God's son, lived and died and rose from the
      grave to save me from my sins, to save me from
      Satan's grasp for now and for all time,
      simply through faith in him. He suffered
      greatly so I wouldn't.

God's grace is mine to accept, to claim, to believe.
      I don't have to earn it. I don't have to be
            "good enough."
      It's free—God's gift to me, to you, to everyone.

God's love permeates all of life.
      His presence is real.
            His peace is deep.
                  His joy is incredible.
God's mercy is great! I am forgiven.

God's faithfulness is sure. He won't leave me even
      if I stray from him. He's always there,
            bringing me back.

God's word is printed in the Bible for me to read
and study for myself; guided by the Holy Spirit,
I find there the presence and presents of God.

God's message is to be shared with all.

Jesus is our model for how to live...
Pray.
Love others, love all.
Take care of other's needs.
Praise God and give him the glory.

The Front Row

Finally, be strong in the Lord and in his mighty power.

Ephesians 6:10

I want to be right up front, Lord,
  where I can see and hear
  all your miracles and all your message.

I want to be right up front, Lord,
  where your table is spread before me
  beckoning, bidding me to
  come and eat,
  come and drink,
  come and be new again in your promise.

I want to be right up front, Lord,
  where I can let it all soak in…
  your love and your sacrifice
  for all, for me.

I want you to be up front in my life, Lord.

Faith Grows

We ought always to thank God for you, brothers and sisters, and rightly so, because your faith is growing more and more, and the love all of you have for one another is increasing.

2 Thessalonians 1:2–4

Faith is a gift that grows as we use it.
Let me step out, Lord,
  in your name
  for your purpose
  in faith.

Let me step out in faith first, Lord,
  then you take over and
  use my hands,
  use my feet,
  use my whole self for your work.

Faith grows, Lord,
  with each day,
  with each time you provide
    skills I never had before and
    courage for the task at hand,
  with each opportunity to serve.

Faith grows—a blessing of the Holy Spirit.

Distractions

Choose this day whom you will serve…but as for me and my household, we will serve the Lord.

Joshua 24:15

Wordsworth was right.
"The world is too much with us."

It's a constant fight
  to stay grounded,
  to stay focused,
  to put Christ first
    in my thoughts,
    in my actions,
    in my life.

So many distractions
  to steal my time and energy,
  to pull me to one side or the other
  away from my center in Christ.

I'm in your hands, Lord.
With you in charge
  I can win the battle
  between your world and mine.

Whose Are You?

But you are a chosen people, a royal priesthood, a holy nation, God's special possession, that you may declare the praises of him who called you out of darkness into his wonderful light.

1 Peter 2:8–10

Who are you? Whose are you?

It's not so important to know who you are
        but to know whose you are is everything.

Are you God's instrument of love and
        service to the world?
Or are you the world's instrument
        mocking service to God?

Are you God's voice of comfort, grace,
        love, and forgiveness to the world?
Or are you the world's voice of "me first,"
        "more toys," "my god is the same as your god"?

Are you God's voice of leadership
        guiding his people
        to unity and salvation   through Jesus Christ?
Or are you the world's style of leadership
        casting doubt on Jesus as our risen Lord
        and savior of all.
Look not at who you are but whose you are.

Dear Lord, help us who are yours
        lead others to be yours too.

| *Joretta K. Klepfer*

Easter

Praise be to the God and Father of our Lord Jesus Christ! In his great mercy he has given us new birth into a living hope through the resurrection of Jesus Christ from the dead,

1 Peter 1:2–4

Going to church

If you're going to pick only one day,
    make it Easter!

The flowers are glorious;
    The music, inspiring.
The altar is dressed;
    The people are smiling.

But, most of all, the message is precious.
Jesus Christ died for you and conquered sin.
Salvation is yours!

Open your heart to Jesus.
His free gift of grace awaits you and
    every Sunday will be an Easter celebration.
Every day will be a new beginning
    of joy, peace, and love in your heart.

Bet you can't pick just one!

Creation Sings God's Glory

My mouth will speak in praise of the Lord.
Let every creature praise his holy name
for ever and ever.

Psalm 145:21

A beautiful morning!

So many avian voices praising God.

So many chattering creatures telling the story
    of God's caretaking.

The rustle of the leaves reveals God's spirit
    in the land.

Blessings of sunshine and cool breezes
    revive me.

Thank you, Lord

Lead Me, Lord

He has shown you, O mortal, what is good.
And what does the Lord require of you?
To act justly and to love mercy
and to walk humbly with your God.

Micah 6:8

Lead me, Lord

What is your direction this day?
Who are the lives that need your touch?
What are the words you want me to say?
How can I show that you love them so much?

A simple poem with profound results
        if I just follow your will.

Thank you, Lord.

Go Forth in Faith

But be sure to fear the Lord and serve him faithfully with
all your heart; consider what great things he has done for
you.

1 Samuel 12:23–25

The mother bird never stops.
She has her task...
    Find a morsel, fly back to the nest.
    Feed the tiny, squeaking baby -
        mouth open and waiting -
        and start all over.

The father bird does the same routine
    but adds one more task to the list.
He calls the little ones to venture forth,
    test their strength, participate in life.

God's metaphor in action -
    Be nurtured and protected.
    Seek his sustenance.
    Then go forth in faith
        to participate in his world.

| *Joretta K. Klepfer*

Washed Clean

For what I received I passed on to you as of first importance:
that Christ died for our sins according to the Scriptures.

1 Corinthians 15:2–4

It's raining today.

The world washed clean is beautiful
      but not more so than a soul
      washed clean with the blood of Christ.

Life-giving water to symbolize life-giving
      blood of Christ, shed for me.

Psalm 23 Litany

The Lord is my shepherd.
> *He leads me.*
> *He guides me.*

I shall not be in want.
> *The food he provides is sufficient and*
> *everlasting.*

He makes me lie down in green pastures.
> *He provides a home for me that*
> *nothing can destroy.*

He leads me beside quiet waters;
he restores my soul.
> *His peace overwhelms all concerns;*
> *problems and cares fall away.*

He guides me in paths of righteousness
for his name's sake.
> *Only his path will take me in the*
> *right direction and lead me closer to him.*

Even though I walk through the valley
of the shadow of death, I will fear no evil.
> *Jesus has conquered Satan for me;*
> *he holds all the power I need.*

For you are with me
> *Always and forever.*

Your rod and your staff, they comfort me.
> *Your guiding hand calms my worries.*

You prepare a table before me in the presence
of my enemies.

> *You have drawn me into your circle of love;*
> *you guide me through all difficulties.*

You anoint my head with oil; my cup overflows.

> *My heart is full; you have blessed me*
> *beyond all measure.*

Surely goodness and love will follow me
all the days of my life

> *Because Jesus walks with me,*
> *ever present, ever faithful.*

And I will dwell in the house of the
Lord forever.

> *May it be so. Amen and amen.*

Remind Me

Your word is a lamp for my feet,
 a light on my path.

Psalm 119:104

Remind me, Lord, that you are ever near me.
Open my mind to learning your word.
Open my ears to hearing your word.
Open my eyes to seeing your word.
Open my heart to receiving your word.
Remind me, Lord, that you are all around me.
Permeate my life with your word.

My Friend

"Come to me, all you who are weary and burdened, and I will give you rest. Take my yoke upon you and learn from me, for I am gentle and humble in heart, and you will find rest for your souls. For my yoke is easy and my burden is light."

Matthew 6:28–30

Have you met my Jesus?
Come with me.

I meet him in the peaceful sunset
    but also in the midst of the storm—
    when the boat rocks and the waves
        crash over the bow;
    when cancer attacks and frequently wins;
    when the loss of a loved one brings
        comfort from a friend.
I meet him in the smiling faces at church but also
        in the crowds where I shop—
    when the tall person reaches the
        top shelf for another;
    when the one checking me out
        also checks in with me;
    when the frustration of lines changes
        to an opportunity to brighten a day;

I meet him on Main Street but also
in the back alleys—
when hot soup and a warm bed welcomes
society's lost ones;
when the kettle rings at Christmas
and the Angel Tree is empty;
when the smiling faces of Habitat volunteers
hand over the keys to a new life.

Have you met my Jesus?
Come with me.
I meet him in every breath,
in every step,
in every thought because he never leaves me.
He is my friend,
my constant companion,
going before me and leading the way.

Have you met my Jesus?
Come with me—he will find you too.

Trusting God

Now faith is confidence in what we hope for and assurance about what we do not see.

Hebrews 11:1–3

Faith…
> A knowing of the heart.
> A reason for my actions.
> Trusting God to love me
>> and keep me close to him.
> Trusting God to give me
>> what I need to face each day.

Washing Windows

Search me, O God, and know my heart;
test me and know my anxious thoughts.
See if there is any offensive way in me,
and lead me in the way everlasting.

Psalm 139:23–24

Washing windows today, Lord
Help me see you clearly.
Through the center pane—your love.
Through the upper panes—your faithfulness.
Through the lower panes—your grace.
Through the entire window—your joy
and light and peace.

Wash the rest of my life clean, Lord.
Open my eyes to the ways I sin
and disappoint you
even when I am not aware of it.
Lead me where you would have me go
and serve you.
Thank you for all your blessings.

Your Promises

For the Lord is good and his love endures forever; his faithfulness continues through all generations.

Psalm 100:4–5

Good morning, Lord
Another day dawns
        with promise—your promise!

Your promise to be by my side.
Your promise of love and grace
        and peace and joy.
Your promise of faithfulness.
Your promise of strength and courage
        for the day ahead.

    Thank you!

My Constant Lifeline

And pray in the Spirit on all occasions with all kinds of
prayers and requests. With this in mind, be alert and always
keep on praying for all the Lord's people.

Ephesians 6:17–19

Prayer
Prayer should be constant.

When is enough, Lord?
A few minutes upon rising?
    Not nearly enough!
A few minutes at bedtime?
    Can't begin to fill my need.

Prayer comes unbidden at times

    when you know I need it.

Prayer is a joyful time of sharing
    moments with you.

Prayer is a tearful time of comfort
    from you.

Prayer is silently reveling in a sunset,
    a soaring bird, a sleeping baby,
    a mother's smile, a father's laughter.

Prayer is my lifeline to you.
Thank you, Lord.

Peace at Last

I pray that the eyes of your heart may be enlightened in order that you may know the hope to which he has called you, the riches of his glorious inheritance in his holy people and his incomparably great power for us who believe.

Ephesians 1:18–19

A day bright and glorious!
    Storms have passed;
God's promise is sure;
    Peace at last!

Lord, you bless us with your presence.
May we be ever aware of your love
        within us and around us.
We need your guidance
        and patience
        and courage
        for the days ahead.

Prepare Me

As for God, his way is perfect: The Lord's word is flawless;
he shields all who take refuge in him.

Psalm 18:29–31

I'm ready, Lord

Prepare my mind to receive
    and understand...

Prepare my heart to listen and obey...

    your Word for all time and
    especially for today.

Did Jesus Doubt?

I do believe; help me overcome my unbelief!

Mark 9:24

Doubts.
So many books tell me I should doubt.
How can I doubt?

Did Jesus doubt?
Did he say,
"I'm not sure he, she, they
        are worth dying for?"
Did he say,
        "Why should I give my life for them?"

No, he died a horrible death
        so that you and I might live.
One sacrifice for all of us.
One life lived—and died—
        for all who believe.

How can I doubt?

His True Story

For what I received I passed on to you as of first importance:
that Christ died for our sins according to the Scriptures, that
he was buried, that he was raised on the third day according
to the Scriptures, and that he appeared to Cephas, and then
to the Twelve.

1 Corinthians 15:3–5

He lives!

For you,
　　　　For me

He suffered;
　　　　He died;
　　　　　　　　He lives again.
For you,
　　　　For me!

He took our sins on himself.

He wiped the slate clean for us.

How can we deny him, saying…
　　　　that it didn't really happen,
　　　　that the Bible is just history?

He was, he is, and ever will be
　　　　the Christ, our Messiah
The Bible is His Story!

Good Morning, Lord

And the peace of God, which transcends all understanding,
will guard your hearts and your minds in Christ Jesus.

Philippians 4:6

Good morning, Lord

The air is still at dawn.
The peace and quiet permeate my soul
    with your presence.

How precious are these early morning times
    with you before your world is awake.

How wonderful to feel so protected
    from all outside.

How thrilling to sit with you
    and seek your word for me.

Thank you.

Star of Jesus

After Jesus was born in Bethlehem in Judea, during the time of King Herod, Magi from the east came to Jerusalem and asked, "Where is the one who has been born king of the Jews? We saw his star when it rose and have come to worship him."

Matthew 2:1–2

Brightly shine, O star of Jesus.

Bring your light to the world.
Announce the birth of the Savior.
Announce your joy for all mankind.
Announce that Jesus' grace, peace,
mercy, and love are ours
to receive,
to accept,
to share.

Brightly shine, O star of Jesus.
Banish darkness for all time.

Come, Receive

"Truly I tell you, anyone who will not receive the kingdom
of God like a little child will never enter it."

Mark 10:15

Like a child
Childlike
We accept
We receive

Faith
Grace
God's gifts to us

Simple
Uncomplicated
He lived for us
He died for us
He went through Hell for us
He lives for us

God says to us…
Come, receive
  my love,
  my grace
    there is no end!

According to Your Word

Behold, I am a servant of the Lord. Let it be to me according
to your word.

Luke 1:38

I seem to be struggling
    with direction, Lord.
I seem to be struggling
    with obedience, Lord.
I seem to be fighting your will
    in favor of my own.

Lord Jesus Christ,
bring clarity to my mind and
    courage to my spirit
    that I may be always
    obedient to your will.

Empower Me

For the Spirit God gave us does not make us timid, but
gives us power, love and self-discipline.

2 Timothy 1:7

Lord, I want my life to bring a smile to your face.

Empower me
>to love you supremely,
>to trust you completely,
>to obey you wholeheartedly today.

Beyond Me

Give thanks to the Lord, for he is good; his love endures forever. The Lord is my strength and my defense; he has become my salvation.

Psalm 118:1, 14

Dear wonderful, incredible Lord Jesus Christ,

Your great power is beyond my imagining.
Thank you for all your miracles on my behalf.

Your great wisdom is beyond my comprehending.
Thank you for your guiding light in my life.

Your great love is beyond my experiencing.
Thank you for your ever present love that
permeates my soul.

Praise

May the peoples praise you, God; may all the peoples praise you. May the nations be glad and sing for joy, f o r you rule the peoples with equity and guide the nations of the earth.

Psalm 67:3–4

PRAISE

I praise you, Lord

P – that I can come to you in Prayer.
R – that you Restore my energy, my joy,
          my life each morning.
A – that you are Always with me—present
          in every day
          in all I do,
          in all I say.
I – that you are Interested in me,
          not just the world in general,
          but in me specifically.
S – that you See me as I am and lead me
          to a better place.
E – that you provide all my Energy
          for living my life for you.

New Year's Day

We wait in hope for the Lord; he is our help and our shield.
In him our hearts rejoice, for we trust in his holy name.

Psalm 33:20–21

A new year, a new life.
      I wait expectantly.
      I wait for God's word.
      I wait for God's will.

The evening sky brings
      the new hope of the waxing moon,
      the promise of order out of chaos,
      the beauty and simplicity
          of God's creation,
      the simple promise of God's
          ever-present love.

Artists and cameras can't do it justice
It must be experienced—just like Jesus!

Show Me, Lord

Therefore, as God's chosen people, holy and dearly loved, clothe yourselves with compassion, kindness, humility, gentleness and patience. Bear with each other and forgive one another if any of you has a grievance against someone. Forgive as the Lord forgave you. And over all these virtues put on love, which binds them all together in perfect unity.

Col 3:12–14

What's the phrase?
Simple act of kindness!
God's love in action.

Hold the door for the shopper
with packages.
Let the driver into traffic
in front of me.
Buy extra cans of food
for the homeless.

I can do those but I can do more.

Open my eyes, Lord,
Show me where,
when,
how
I can put your love into action.

Help me keep my life focused
on serving you
by serving others.

God Come Down

But the angel said to them, "Do not be afraid. I bring you good news that will cause great joy for all the people. Today in the town of David a Savior has been born to you; he is the Messiah, the Lord.

Luke 2:10–11

The Christmas tree still glows with
    multicolored lights.
The Chrismon tree tells the story
    in white and gold.

Christ the King has come to earth.
Christ, the Savior of all, is among us.

Christ will not leave us when the
    holiday reminders are put away.

The blessing of "God come down"
    is ever present.

Joretta K. Klepfer

Keep Me Focused

But as for me and my household, we will serve the Lord.

Joshua 24:15b

A new day at work.
A new year at work.
Whose work, Lord?
 Mine or yours?

Let me be ever aware of opportunities
 to serve you
 whenever I can,
 whomever I meet.

Any service however small may be huge
 to the recipient.

Help me stay focused on your work, Lord.

Slow Me Down

Day after day, in the temple courts and from house to house,
they never stopped teaching and proclaiming the good news
that Jesus is the Messiah.

Acts 5:42

It's Wednesday, Jesus.

The week is flying by.

Slow me down.
>Help me listen to your word.
>Help me be aware of each moment in the day.
>Show me how I can reach out in your name.

Let me not miss an opportunity to share the
good news of your grace and peace.

Peace and Joy

But the Advocate, the Holy Spirit, whom the Father will send in my name, will teach you all things and will remind you of everything I have said to you.

John 14:26

I prayed but I didn't write yesterday.

I think I probably prayed more than I realize
      since the Holy Spirit is always
      looking out for me.

Sometimes there is just such
      a feeling of peace and joy.

What gifts!
What blessing, Lord.
Thank you!

I Believe, Lord

And this is his command: to believe in the name of his Son,
Jesus Christ, and to love one another as he commanded us.
The one who keeps God's commands lives in him, and he
in them. And this is how we know that he lives in us: We
know it by the Spirit he gave us.

1 John 3:23–24

Should I be questioning, Lord?
What's wrong with simply believing
    that you know what's best for me,
    that you are always with me,
    that you love me more than I can possibly
        understand,
    that you understand my misunderstanding,
    that you forgive me over and over again,
    that you died for me to wipe out the stain
        of my sins for all eternity?
I believe, Lord!
    that you created me and all that exists;
    that you are still creating;
    that you came to earth in our own form
        and your name was, and is, Jesus;
    that you died for all sins for all time
        because we are bound by sin;
    that you live in me today through your
        Holy Spirit.
What a blessing!
Your joy and peace are mine to claim today.
Thank you!

Monday Morning

And this is my prayer: that your love may abound more and more in knowledge and depth of insight, so that you may be able to discern what is best and may be pure and blameless for the day of Christ, filled with the fruit of righteousness that comes through Jesus Christ—to the glory and praise of God.

Philippians 1:9–11

It's Monday morning.
Coffee is the word for the day.

What happened to the weekend?
I had so much I wanted to accomplish.

I think you answered my prayer, Lord.
You helped me take care of the important stuff
        and let the rest wait another day.
Thank you.

Forgiveness

Therefore, my friends, I want you to know that through Jesus the forgiveness of sins is proclaimed to you. Through him everyone who believes is set free from every sin, a justification you were not able to obtain under the law of Moses.

Acts 13:38-39

Forgiveness—a powerful word, Lord.

In Christ, you have given me the greatest
    gifts of all—
        grace,
        mercy,
        forgiveness.

What comfort and peace your great love
    brings to me.

You don't hold my sins against me.
Thank you.

True Joy

As the Father has loved me, so have I loved you. Now remain in my love. If you keep my commands, you will remain in my love, just as I have kept my Father's commands and remain in his love. I have told you this so that my joy may be in you and that your joy may be complete.

John 15:9–11

JOY!

A fleeting concept?

No, rather a constant presence within my soul.

Because its source is from Jesus Christ.

Only in Christ do I know true joy.

Jesus Cleanses Me

Create in me a pure heart, O God, and renew a steadfast
spirit within me.

Psalm 51:10

Snow.
You have cleaned my world this morning, Lord.

Would that hearts be cleansed so easily.
Send your Holy Spirit to seek out the dark corners
       of my life,
       of my world,
       and make them pure and whole.

Thank you for Jesus who wiped the slate
       clean for me.

Light of Christ

The people walking in darkness have seen a great light;
on those living in the land of deep darkness a light has
dawned.

Isaiah 9:2

Shine your light for me, Lord.
Help me see through the darkness.
Illumine the path you have planned for me
      and let me not step away from it.
Help me share your light with those
      also in dark corners.

Come, Lord Jesus

Surely you have granted him unending blessings and made
him glad with the joy of your presence.

Psalm 21:6

Come, Lord Jesus.
Sit with me a while.

Enjoy the peace, the quiet of the early morning.
Share your stories with me.
Guide me to more faithful understanding
        of your word.
Let the world fall away.
Lead me deeper and deeper into your heart
        that I may drown myself in your love.

My Light for Living

I will lead the blind by ways they have not known, along unfamiliar paths I will guide them; I will turn the darkness into light before them and make the rough places smooth. These are the things I will do; I will not forsake them.

Isaiah 42:16

You are my light, Lord,
     guiding me,
     leading me,
     showing me the way I should go.

Give me the courage to follow.
Give me the faith to quash my fear and doubt.

For your precious gifts of
     grace and
     mercy and
     love and
     peace and
     faith,
I thank you.

Patience!

I waited patiently for the Lord; he turned to me and heard
my cry.

Psalm 40:1

Patience!

I seem to have lost your gift to me, Lord.

Help me to know the value of waiting,
    of stilling my desires in favor of yours,
    of looking for your timing of things.

Holy Spirit, your gift of patience is precious.

Please help me find your gift to me again,
    and this time not lose it!

Joretta K. Klepfer

Jesus Loves Me

Jesus replied, "Anyone who loves me will obey my teaching. My Father will love them, and we will come to them and make our home with them.

John 14:22–24

Jesus loves me, this I know
    because I feel his loving presence
        surrounding me,
    because I see him every day in
        everyone I meet.
    Would that they could see him too.

Jesus loves me.
    I feel his peace deep inside.
    I see his smile.
    I hear his laughter.
    I feel his gentle touch as I am
        surrounded by people
        he has touched.

Lord Jesus, please use me to show
    you to others.

My Bible

And we also thank God continually because, when you received the word of God, which you heard from us, you accepted it not as a human word, but as it actually is, the word of God, which is indeed at work in you who believe.

1 Thessalonians 2:13

The song says it best.
>"Jesus loves me, this I know
>for the Bible tells me so."

I trust your word, Lord.

I love being able to read it for myself
>and glean your truth from it.

I love the peace and comfort I feel
>while reading it.

Thank you for this precious gift.

Wash the Dust from My Life

You make known to me the path of life; you will fill me with joy in your presence, with eternal pleasures at your right hand.

Psalm 16:11

A rainy day.

Refresh me, Lord,
    like you have refreshed our world.

Wash away the dust of
    sin,
    worry,
    impatience,
    doubt,
    and all those things which
    keep me from seeing you clearly.

Help me to walk in the path you choose for me
    through the bright clean world you provide.

Spring

But when the kindness and love of God our Savior appeared, he saved us, not because of righteous things we had done, but because of his mercy. He saved us through the washing of rebirth and renewal by the Holy Spirit, whom he poured out on us generously through Jesus Christ our Savior, so that, having been justified by his grace, we might become heirs having the hope of eternal life.

Titus 3:4–7

It's April!

The earth awakens once again
      with all of the colors of God's rainbow.

A promise kept.
The old dying away.
A new world bursting forth in beauty
      more and more every day.

We are blessed.
Thank you, Lord.

Let there also be your presence anew
      in each heart.

Restores My Soul

I will praise you with the harp or your faithfulness, my God;
I will sing praise to you with the lyre, Holy One of Israel.
My lips will shout for joy when I sing praise to you—I
whom you have delivered.

Psalm 71:22–23

The birds sing, "Hallelujah."
The squirrels chatter, "Praise God."

It's that kind of morning!

Spring brings renewal to our world and
        restores my soul.
Once again, there's a new creation.

Thank you, Lord.

Let Your Light Shine Through

A new command I give you: Love one another. As I have loved you, so you must love one another. By this everyone will know that you are my disciples, if you love one another.

John 13:34–35

Be my window, Lord.

Let me see the world through your eyes
> of love,
> of concern,
> of compassion,
> of friendship.

Be my window, Lord.

Let your light stream through to brighten
> every corner of my life.

Show me where, when, how
> I can share your light.

Spring Magic

The whole earth is filled with awe at your wonders;
where morning dawns, where evening fades, you call forth
songs of joy.

Psalm 65:8

The magic is back.

Each spring brings its own proof of God's
      power of creation.

You make our world new again, Lord.
You don't stop with just one shade of green
      or yellow or red or purple or blue.

Thank you.

Help Us, Lord

They also will answer, 'Lord, when did we see you hungry or thirsty or a stranger or needing clothes or sick or in prison, and did not help you?' He will reply, 'Truly I tell you, whatever you did not do for one of the least of these, you did not do for me.'

Matthew 25:44–45

The birds are singing.
The sun is shining warm and glorious
      on the colors of spring.
All's right with the world.

But is it really?

It's not right that people are hungry,
      even starving.
It's not right that people are homeless.
It's not right that people are helpless to fight
      their circumstances while others look on
      casually, uncaringly.
It's not right until all are clothed, fed,
      and housed.

Help us, Lord.
Help us make it right.

Jesus, My Friend

Because I live, you also will live. On that day you will realize that I am in my Father, and you are in me, and I am in you. Whoever has my commands and keeps them is the one who loves me. The one who loves me will be loved by my Father, and I too will love them and show myself to them."

John 14:19b–21

Jesus, my friend,
      walks beside me through the day.

Jesus, my friend,
      listens to my concerns and complaints.

Jesus, my friend,
      laughs with me through foibles
      and troubles.

Jesus, my friend,
      guides me into a deeper abiding love
      for him, for all.

Jesus, my friend,
      sits with me in the quiet and in the chaos.

Jesus, my friend,
      shares the beauty and joy of my life.

With Joy and Enthusiasm

May the God of hope fill you with all joy and peace as you trust in him, so that you may overflow with hope by the power of the Holy Spirit.

Romans 15:13

Dear Lord Jesus,

With joy and enthusiasm,
     let me share your word.

With joy and enthusiasm,
     let me share your love.

With joy and enthusiasm,
     let me greet your children in the world.

With joy and enthusiasm,
     let me serve you in all that I do
     every day,
     everywhere I go.

Joretta K. Klepfer

Knocking on Hearts

Here I am! I stand at the door and knock. If anyone hears my voice and opens the door, I will come in and eat with that person, and they with me.

Revelation 3:20

The woodpecker announces the morning,
        echoing through the woods
        knocking, knocking as he flies from
        one tree to another
        just like Jesus knocking on heart after heart.

How many will let him in?

How many will surrender themselves to him -
        their whole selves -
        to do his work,
        to share his love,
        in the world?

Joy

If you then, though you are evil, know how to give good gifts to your children, how much more will your Father in heaven give the Holy Spirit to those who ask him!"

Luke 11:13

A joyous life,
    A happy spirit.
Your gifts, O Lord.
    Let me never forget.

Hear My Prayer

As the deer pants for streams of water, so my soul pants for you, my God. My soul thirsts for God, for the living God.

Psalm 42:1–2a

I need you, Lord,
    every minute
    of every day.

Hear my prayer for your presence
    as I sleep,
    as I work,
    in my poor attempt to be Christlike.

Sustain the yearning for you in my heart.

The Better Choice

Rejoice in the Lord always. I will say it again: Rejoice! Let your gentleness be evident to all. The Lord is near. Do not be anxious about anything, but in every situation, by prayer and petition, with thanksgiving, present your requests to God. And the peace of God, which transcends all understanding, will guard your hearts and your minds in Christ Jesus.

Philippians 4:4–7

Worry takes your life and
    turns it over to the world.
    You're trapped in a downward spiral.

Prayer takes your worry and
    turns it over to God.
    You're free.

Better choice -
    Just pray!

My Father

Abba, Father, he said, everything is possible for you. Take
this cup from me. Yet not what I will, but what you will.

Mark 14:36

Jesus called you Father and that's
    good enough for me.
So you are my Father, too

Jesus showed me the way so
    I can think of you as "he."
    I can speak of you as "he"
    and I shall!

Thank you, Father God.

Sun Breaks Through

Blessed is the one… whose delight is in the law of the
Lord, and who meditates on his law day and night.

Psalm 1:1–2

I sit with clouds hanging low overhead
    pondering the day,
    trying to keep worry at bay.

The sun breaks through with God's bright light
    chasing all doubts far away.

God's Way For Me

Show me your ways, Lord, teach me your paths. Guide me in your truth and teach me, for you are God my Savior, and my hope is in you all day long.

Psalm 25:4–5

What is truth, Lord?

Help me see clearly.

Help me keep my ideas, longings, desires
    from taking over.

Help me accept and adopt your truth,
    your way for me.

God's Hand on My Shoulder

I will praise the Lord, who counsels me; even at night my
heart instructs me. I keep my eyes always on the Lord.
With him at my right hand, I will not be shaken.

Psalm 16:7–8

I'll walk down this path, Lord,
knowing you'll walk beside me.

Keep your hand on my shoulder
guiding each step.

Let me see what you see;
let me hear what you hear
that I might serve you
by serving those you love.

Help me to love them too.

A Vessel of Your Love

Dear friends, since God so loved us, we also ought to love one another. No one has ever seen God; but if we love one another, God lives in us and his love is made complete in us.

1 John 4:11–12

A clean page, Lord,
    a clean slate
    you offer to me each day.

O, that I may use it to serve you.

Make me a vessel
    pouring out your love
    on all around me,
    close or far.

Once for All

Just as people are destined to die once, and after that to face judgment, so Christ was sacrificed once to take away the sins of many; and he will appear a second time, not to bear sin, but to bring salvation to those who are waiting for him.

Hebrews 9:27–28

Once for all.

A simple phrase, Lord,
> but profound in meaning.

You died to save all mankind,
> all of us
> for all time,
> for me!

My sins are forgiven by the sacrifice you made
> for me!

Thank you.

God Won

If any of you lacks wisdom, you should ask God, who gives generously to all without finding fault, and it will be given to you. But when you ask, you must believe and not doubt, because the one who doubts is like a wave of the sea, blown and tossed by the wind.

James 1:5–6

The Christmas season is upon us with all its
      beauty and peace.
Your gift to us, Lord Jesus,
      a time to celebrate your birth.

Some say you must have been born in the
      spring instead of winter.

Does it really matter if we celebrate December 25
      instead of March 25?
Does it really matter if the date was picked
      because of a pagan celebration?
YOU WON!

Where is that pagan celebration now?
What was it then?
Does anyone remember anything happening
      other than your birth?
Help the doubters find peace, Lord.
      Be in their hearts.
      Guide them.
      Love them.

A New Year!

'For in him we live and move and have our being.'

Acts 17:28a

A new year!

New days to live for you, Lord.

May these be the days that I serve you best,
> each one more focused than the one before,
>> focused on serving you,
>> focused on serving others,
>> focused on studying your word,
>> focused on loving you and others.

Faithful Acceptance

Now faith is confidence in what we hope for and assurance
about what we do not see.

Hebrews 11:1

Forgive my doubts, Lord.

Every time I start to question how
      I, my family, the world came to be,
      remind me that I don't have to understand,
      that you don't expect me to understand.

All you ask is that I just accept in faith
      that you created me and all that exists,
      that you sent Jesus to die for me,
      that your love is beyond all imagining.

Sharing His Love

But because of his great love for us, God, who is rich in
mercy, made us alive with Christ even when we were dead
in transgressions—it is by grace you have been saved.

Ephesians 2:4–5

Alive in Christ!
What does that mean?
Living my life for him, not me.
Living with passion and energy
        to share his word,
        to share his love
        even on days when I'm tired,
            bone-weary,
        even on days when I'm angry,
            sad, depressed.
Christ gives me the energy to live for him
        to put my focus on him and not me.

So what can I do to live for him?
How can I start?

Simply at first…
        Christ habits will become ingrained.
        Live from the heart.
        Smile at the clerk.
        Open the door for someone.
        Pick up a child's toy for the stressed out
            mother with arms full of children.
        Take care of my family with joy not duty.

Look around!
The more I look, the more opportunities I will find
to be "others-centered,"
to focus on living in the image of Christ.

Focused on You, Lord

And we know that in all things God works for the good of those who love him, who have been called according to his purpose.

Romans 8:28

The year advances rapidly.
Morning becomes night in a bright flash.

How many opportunities are lost when I don't
        stay focused.

Keep me lined up with your purpose, Lord.
Keep me tuned in to your will.

Each day of winter brings more light.
Each day focused on you brings more light, too,
        to my spirit,
        to my life.

Like a Child

Truly I tell you, anyone who will not receive the kingdom
of God like a little child will never enter it."

Luke 15:17

There is nothing simple about faith
and yet, there it is.

Faith like a child, simple faith,
is a knowing of the heart,
a knowing of Jesus Christ.

It is past believing of the head.
It is a knowing that comes from living with Jesus
in my heart,
my head,
my whole self,
directing my steps,
my thoughts,
my actions.

It is a knowing so deep that I don't have
to think about it.
It is just there
in the midst of everything I do, I think, I am.

Thank you, Lord, for this wonderful gift.

Reflection Time

May these words of my mouth and this meditation of my
heart be pleasing in your sight, Lord, my Rock and my Redeemer.

Psalm 19:14

Early Saturday morning,
     a treasure of quiet reflection time
     of listening to the birds in their
          pre-dawn singing,
     of watching the beautiful colors of dawn,
     of the joy of God's presence.

How do I say, "Thank you," Lord?

How do I pay for such pleasure?
     By believing and sharing your love,
     By believing and sharing your son, Jesus,
     By believing and sharing your Spirit

Snow

Blessed are those whose transgressions are forgiven,
whose sins are covered. Blessed is the one whose sin the
Lord will never count against them.

Romans 4:7–8

Overnight, the world outside is white.
How magical!

The dark has vanished under a coat of fresh
    white powder.

The silence of the dawn invites wonder as a child,
    just the way we come to God
        in wonder at the gift of his son,
        in joy as Jesus has lived for us,
        in thankfulness as Jesus died for our sins,
        in simple faith.

Jesus has covered our sins
    and made them disappear like the dark
    under the snow.

Open My Eyes

Be very careful, then, how you live—not as unwise but as wise, making the most of every opportunity, because the days are evil. Therefore do not be foolish, but understand what the Lord's will is.

Ephesians 5:15–17

Thank you for this day, Lord.

Help me see the ways I can serve you.

Open my eyes to habits that are keeping me
  distant from you.
Open my eyes to opportunities I've missed
  to share your word,
  to share your love.

Keep me ever aware of your presence.
Keep me close to your will
  and let me not stray from it.

Believing Is the Answer

Then Jesus told him, "Because you have seen me, you have believed; blessed are those who have not seen and yet have believed."

John 20:29

I catch myself asking, "How?"

How could God be three persons in one being?
How could he be all things to all people at all times?
When the question I should be asking is, "Why?"
Why? Because he loves me,
  because he loves you
  and just keeps on looking after us.
  He's with each one of us every second
    of every minute
    of every hour
    of every day
    of every year.
I strive to remember that when I have doubts.
I strive to share his good news with others who
  have doubts.
I just remember,
  "Jesus loves me, this I know"
  in my heart,
  in my whole being.
Understanding is not expected and
  certainly not required and
  definitely not necessary.

Believing IS!
Believing leads me into a personal relationship
    with my creator,
    with my savior,
    with my friend.

Believing leads me
    to love,
    to forgive,
    to reach out with no expectation of return,
    to live with Jesus at the center of my life
    always and forever.

Stand Up for Jesus

For we did not follow cleverly devised stories when we told you about the coming of our Lord Jesus Christ in power, but we were eyewitnesses of his majesty. For prophecy never had its origin in the human will, but prophets, though human, spoke from God as they were carried along by the Holy Spirit.

2 Peter 16, 21

Simple faith is being bombarded.

The church today is filled with false prophets
    who tear down the authority of scripture
    in subtle, insidious ways.

False prophets...
    among us now as they were so many years ago,
    spreading seeds of doubt,
    nurturing the weeds that follow.
Lord Jesus Christ, grant me clarity of mind
    and heart
    to see you in all that I do,
    to understand your will for me.
Grant me courage to speak out in your name.
Guide my thoughts, my words, my actions
    that I might be a true witness for you
    to the world.
Guide me, Lord, to know your truth.
Guide me that I may live in your truth and
    be faithful to it.

The Simple Things

So then, just as you received Christ Jesus as Lord,
continue to live your lives in him, rooted and built up in
him, strengthened in the faith as you were taught, and
overflowing with thankfulness.

Colossians 2:6–7

Life.

It all comes down to the simple things.

What shall I eat for my next meal?
       Where will I find it?
       If you know, be grateful and thank God.

What shall I wear today?
       If you have a choice, thank God.

Where shall I sleep tonight?
       If you know, thank God.
       If you have a bed, thank God.

Where shall I find shelter for my family?
       If it is in your own home,
       your space for you and your family,
       thank God even more.

Thank God and share
       so that all may enjoy the simple things.
But, most of all, share Jesus
       so that all may know life's source.

Live with Faith

Grace and peace be yours in abundance through the knowledge of God and of Jesus our Lord. His divine power has given us everything we need for a godly life through our knowledge of him who called us by his own glory and goodness.

2 Peter 1:2–3

Life is precious.

Live with purpose.

Live with faith.

Live with the awareness
    that all you are
    and all you have
    come from God.

Good Friday

To the Jews who had believed him, Jesus said, "If you hold
to my teaching, you are really my disciples. Then you will
know the truth, and the truth will set you free."

John 8:31–32

Were you there?

"Were you there when they crucified my Lord?"
A truly special hymn, and the question is
    still relevant.

Were you there...

when others were mocking Christianity
    and you stood silent?
when others took Christ's name in vain
    and you stood silent?
when others drove by the homeless man
    and you did too?

When "false prophets" tear down scripture,
    denying the truth of Christ,
    do you sit quietly, listening and doing nothing?

I am convicted, Lord.
I beg your forgiveness for my poor witness
    to your truth.

What Do We Reap?

We wait in hope for the Lord; he is our help and our shield.
In him our hearts rejoice, or we trust in his holy name. May
your unfailing love be with us, Lord, even as we put our
hope in you.

Psalm 33:20–22

We reap what we sow.

Have we nurtured faith, with which comes
        peace, joy, and passionate spirituality
        resting in God's grace?

Or have we nurtured doubt, with which comes
        unrest, questioning every move,
        having no foundation,
        trying to earn God's love?

In No Uncertain Terms

I will praise the Lord, who counsels me; even at night my
heart instructs me. I keep my eyes always on the Lord.
With him at my right hand, I will not be shaken.

Psalm 16:7–8

Good morning, Lord.
Thank you for this day.

Help me use it your way, not mine.
Show me your will for my life
      what's the phrase?
      "in no uncertain terms!"
(Please nothing obscure lest I miss the
      opportunity by the time I catch on.)
Then give me the courage to follow!

You lead the way and I can be at peace in you.

Time to Be

Yes, my soul, find rest in God; my hope comes from him.
Truly he is my rock and my salvation;

Psalm 62:5–6a

Another Saturday morning stretches before me.
Time to relax in your word, Lord.

Thank you for the time
        to read,
        to study,
        to pray,
        to reflect
        about all you have done for me
        so that I may be grateful for faith
        and thankful for your blessings.

Details

While they were eating, Jesus took bread, and when he had given thanks, he broke it and gave it to his disciples, saying, "Take it; this is my body." Then he took a cup, and when he had given thanks, he gave it to them, and they all drank from it. "This is my blood of the covenant, which is poured out for many," he said to them.

Mark 14:22–24

Details!

The old saying is true if we are drawn
        to argue incessantly over details such as
        what was served at the Passover meal;
        whether the Last Supper was indeed a Passover meal;
        why no mention of a sacrificial lamb?

What more do we need to know than
        Jesus himself was the sacrificial lamb?

Jesus died to wipe away all sins for all time
        for those who accept this incredible gift.

What more do we need to know?

A New Day

God is light; in him there is no darkness at all. ... if we walk in the light, as he is in the light, we have fellowship with one another, and the blood of Jesus, his Son, purifies us from all sin.

1 John 1:5,7

A new day, Lord.

Your sunshine brightens every corner
                of my world
        just like your Son brings light
        to every corner of my heart
        with peace,
        with joy,
        with love.

Thank you.

Trust Me

"For I know the plans I have for you," declares the Lord, "plans to prosper you and not to harm you, plans to give you hope and a future."

Jeremiah 29:11

My word from God this morning…

"Be ready and wait!
I will come to you on my terms.
I will reveal my will for you in my own way.
Trust me!
Trust my plan I have for you.
You're in good hands—so relax."

Write!

Finally, be strong in the Lord and in his mighty power.

Ephesians 6:10

God's message for me this morning…

"Write!
Pick up your pencil, pen, laptop, and write!
Write the words I tell you.

Write about
      my love for you and all mankind,
      my grace that is free for all who believe,
      my concern for the world I created,
          how you have neglected its care,
      my anger that you are still killing one another.

Just because I gave you free will, doesn't mean
      you should let the devil take over your lives.
You have to fight.
You have to be strong.
I will give you the strength you need -
      you have but to ask.
I want you to want to be with me,
      to want to do my will,
      to want a relationship with me.

I love you."

A New Creation

Therefore, if anyone is in Christ, the new creation has come: The old has gone, the new is here!

2 Corinthians 5:17

God rested on the seventh day.

He didn't stop creating.
He didn't stop forming and re-forming.

When we let his creation go awry
      he sent his Son, Jesus,
        to provide a whole new creation within us.

Friends

Dear friends, let us love one another, for love comes from God. Everyone who loves has been born of God and knows God.

1 John 4:7

Friends.

God gave us one another
    to be his arms of encircling love;
    to be his hands carrying food to the sick,
        the poor, the lonely;
    to be his voice of soothing, caring concern
        to the sick, the poor,
        the lonely, the broken;
    to be his ear for listening to the sick,
        the poor, the lonely, the broken,
        the lost.
God gave us one another—all of us,
    the people of earth
        not just those we know,
        not just those we like,
        not just those we are like,
    and definitely not just those who already
    know him.

We must share his love
    and his message of Christ, our salvation,
    with all we meet.
We are his tools in the world
    for doing his work.

Keep Me Alert

Then Jesus said to his disciples, "Whoever wants to be my disciple must deny themselves and take up their cross and follow me. For whoever wants to save their life will lose it, but whoever loses their life for me will find it.

Matthew 16:24–25

Time marches on.

What did I do for you today, Lord?
What opportunity to serve did I pass up,
          not recognize, feel too busy to do?

Keep me ever watchful for ways to serve you.
Keep me ever aware of your presence.
Open my eyes.
          Open my heart.
                    Give me courage to act.

Time marches on!
Help me spend it serving you.
Let my days not be wasteful.
Let my days be always prayerful.

Stand Up

For the Spirit God gave us does not make us timid, but gives us power, love and self-discipline.

2 Timothy 1:7

Posture is prayer.

Stand up for Jesus.

Stand straight in your faith
  not slumped over in doubt.

Stand straight for the world to see
  the joy of God's love,
  the joy of God's peace
  in the midst of the chaos of everyday.

Lift your head in strong belief of God's
  presence and blessing in your life.

Lift your head in the sure confidence
  that God is real
  and your basis for living.

Lift your head in the sure confidence
  that you are not alone.

He is with you in everything you do.

Rain

Praise be to the God and Father of our Lord Jesus Christ, who has blessed us in the heavenly realms with every spiritual blessing in Christ.

Ephesians 1:3

Blessed rain.

Life-giving rain.
Fall upon us like the shower of God's blessings.

Thank you, Lord, for breaking the drought
in our world.

Thank you, Lord, for breaking the drought
in our lives.

Seek Jesus

And without faith it is impossible to please God, because anyone who comes to him must believe that he exists and that he rewards those who earnestly seek him.

Hebrews 11:6

Pray with purpose!

Seek to know Jesus.
Seek to be his disciple.

Praise him.
Thank him.
Ask forgiveness.
Bask in his presence.

Seek not to understand but to accept
        the majesty of Father, Son, and Holy Spirit.
Seek to accept his gift of faith.

Seek to know God
        in all his glory and majesty and power,
        in all his love
        and gentleness
        and faithfulness.

Faith Is a Gift

Therefore, since we have been justified through faith, we have peace with God through our Lord Jesus Christ, through whom we have gained access by faith into this grace in which we now stand. And we boast in the hope of the glory of God.

Romans 5:1–2

By faith,
>I walk with God each day.

By faith,
>I feel his loving presence.

By faith,
>I know no doubts
>>about God, my father;
>>about Jesus, my Savior;
>>about the Holy Spirit,
>>my guide through life.

Even a slight flicker of questioning
>is quickly dispelled
>because I don't have
>to understand to believe.

My faith is a gift from God
>through Jesus and the Holy Spirit.
How wonderful to be so blessed.

Thank you, Lord.

For Such a Time As This

And who knows but that you have come to your royal position for such a time as this?"

Esther 4:14b

Lord, you have brought me
    to this time, this place
    to share your truth,
    to share your word for the world.

Your word
    not the message mankind has distorted.

Your truth
    not the distortions mankind has produced.

May we all accept
    and believe
    and share your gifts of faith.

Mercy

But because of his great love for us, God, who is rich in mercy, made us alive with Christ even when we were dead in transgressions—it is by grace you have been saved.

Ephesians 2:4–5

Lord Jesus Christ,

Your mercy is great
        my response, too little
        but thank you for forgiving my sins.

Your love is omnipresent and compelling
        my response, too narrow and selfish
        but thank you for showering me with love.

My Protector, Role Model, Friend

The Lord is my rock, my fortress and my deliverer; my God is my rock, in whom I take refuge, my shield and the horn of my salvation, my stronghold.

Psalm 18:2

Dear Lord Jesus,

You are my
protector,
role model,
friend.

You help me pick up the pieces
when I turn my life upside down.

You show me the way
to be kind, loving, joyful.

Help me to live up to your example.

You provide the light for my life.
You take away the darkness.

Thank you.

Time

For none of us lives for ourselves alone, and none of us dies for ourselves alone. If we live, we live for the Lord; and if we die, we die for the Lord. So, whether we live or die, we belong to the Lord.

Romans 14:7–8

Time slips by.

Another day,
      another week,
            another month,
                  another year.

Past, before I know it as today,
      the future is upon me.

How have I used my time, Lord,
      your time, your gift to me?

Make me open to using each minute
      of every day
      to honor you,
      to praise you,
      to give you the glory,
      for all that I do.

God Is Good

Then Jesus declared, "I am the bread of life. Whoever comes to me will never go hungry, and whoever believes in me will never be thirsty."

John 6:35

The saying "Life is good" is showing
    up everywhere these days.

On the contrary,
    life is life.
    God is good!

Life is a precious gift from God.
Honor it.
Preserve it.
Be thankful.

Freedom

Now the Lord is the Spirit, and where the Spirit of the Lord is, there is freedom. And we all, who with unveiled faces contemplate the Lord's glory, are being transformed into his image with ever-increasing glory, which comes from the Lord, who is the Spirit.

2 Corinthians 3:17–18

Freedom
>   a precious gift from God
>   through the courageous
>   who went before,
>
>   a responsibility for us to tend each day,
>
>   a legacy to bless those who come after.

Praise God from Whom All Blessings Flow

Praise God in his sanctuary; praise him in his mighty heavens. Praise him for his acts of power; praise him for his surpassing greatness. Let everything that has breath praise the Lord.

Psalm 150:1–2,6

"Praise God from whom all blessings flow."
An old song, well loved, still relevant,
and a reminder to be grateful
for all that I have,
for all that I am,
for all that I will be.

Lord, I praise you.
Monday, I praise you for your incredible,
spectacular, breathtaking creation.

Tuesday, I praise you for your wonderful
love that surrounds me and picks me up.

Wednesday, I praise you for healing
my body, my spirit, my soul.

Thursday, I praise you for your faithfulness.
You are always there for me.

Friday, I praise you for your never-failing
mercy and forgiveness.

Saturday, I praise you for your never-ending
patience with me.

Sunday, I praise you for everything
and give you glory,
my Father God, everlasting.

Amen and amen.

Saturday Morning

The Lord Almighty is with us; the God of Jacob is our fortress. He says, "Be still, and know that I am God;

Psalm 46:7, 10a

Saturday morning!

All is quiet,
> no school bus tires squeaking outside,
> no chainsaws going yet,
> only the AC makes a sound,
> trying its best to stave off the oppressive heat.

Saturday morning, Lord.
Extra time to rest in you,
> to be still and revel in your presence,
> to be in you.

I am blessed.
Thank you.

Sighs

In the same way, the Spirit helps us in our weakness. We do not know what we ought to pray for, but the Spirit himself intercedes for us through wordless groans. And he who searches our hearts knows the mind of the Spirit, because the Spirit intercedes for God's people in accordance with the will of God.

Romans 8:26–27

A child thrown away.

A life destroyed by alcohol or drugs.

Anger that overwhelms judgment.

Senseless shootings

Disease that replaces life's joys
    with pain and frustration.

The Spirit intercedes
    when my sighs are too deep for words.

| *Joretta K. Klepfer*

Thank You for This Day

I pray that your partnership with us in the faith may be effective in deepening your understanding of every good thing we share for the sake of Christ.

Philemon 1:6

Dear Lord,

Thank you for this day.
>Help me use it for you.

Thank you for this day.
>Help me share your love.

Thank you for this day.
>Help me know your peace.

Thank you for this day.
>Help me share your joy.

Be with Me

And do not forget to do good and to share with others, for
with such sacrifices God is pleased.

Hebrews 13:16

Be ever in my heart, Lord Jesus.
Be ever in my mind.
Be ever on my lips, Lord Jesus,
Ever loving, ever kind,
Sharing your love with all.

Settle Me, Focus Me, Teach Me

Finally, brothers and sisters, whatever is true, whatever is noble, whatever is right, whatever is pure, whatever is lovely, whatever is admirable—if anything is excellent or praiseworthy—think about such things. Whatever you have learned or received or heard from me, or seen in me—put it into practice. And the God of peace will be with you.

Philippians 4:8–9

Lord Jesus Christ,

As I pick up my Bible, my prayer is
    settle me down,
    focus my mind,
    teach me through your word.

As I go about my day my prayer is
    keep me focused on your word for me,
    wherever I am,
    whomever I meet.

May I always expect to meet you.

Life As a Prayer

Rejoice always, pray continually, give thanks in all circumstances; for this is God's will for you in Christ Jesus.

1 Thessalonians 5:16–18

Lord in your mercy, hear my prayer.

Let all my life be a prayer to you
      every minute of my day,
      every day of my week,
      every week of my year,
      every year of my life.

Not my will Lord, but yours!

Show Me How

Let the morning bring me word of your unfailing love, for I have put my trust in you. Show me the way I should go, for to you I entrust my life.

Psalm 143:8

Show me each day, Lord,
    how to serve you.

Show me each day, Lord,
    how to stay focused on you.

Show me each day, Lord,
    the steps I should take.

Show me each day, Lord,
    how to live in your will.

Show me each day, Lord,
    for I am lost without you.

Give Me Courage

You make known to me the path of life; you will fill me with joy in your presence, with eternal pleasures at your right hand.

Psalm 16:11

Good morning, Lord.

The day is bright with
        new promise,
        new excitement,
        new joy.

Thank you.

May the year ahead be yours, not mine.

Help me meet the challenges you present.

Give me the courage to walk the path you
        choose for me.

A Clean Heart

Search me, O God, and know my heart; test me and know
my anxious thoughts. See if there is any offensive way in
me and lead me in the way everlasting.

Psalm 139:23–24

My daily prayer from scripture, O Lord.
Let no sin reside in me that is not
    confessed and repented.
"Create in me a clean heart."

Come and See

"Come and see"

John 1:46

Come and see Jesus.
    See with your heart
        that Jesus loves you.
    See with your mind
        what Jesus teaches you.
    See with your eyes
        what Jesus created for you.
    See with your spirit
        that his Spirit never leaves you.

Guiding, Leading, Teaching

The Lord himself goes before you and will be with you; he will never leave you nor forsake you. Do not be afraid; do not be discouraged."

Deuteronomy 31:8

January 31

The last day of the first month.

I praise you, Lord, that you stay with me
       through all,
       each day and every day.

I know you are near
       guiding me through the rough spots,
       leading me down your path for me,
       teaching me your ways.

Accept Jesus

Praise be to the God and Father of our Lord Jesus Christ, who has blessed us in the heavenly realms with every spiritual blessing in Christ.

Ephesians 1:3

It's so simple.

We have heaven in our grasp
       just love Jesus and accept his sacrifice
       for you
       for me.

Live for him.
Live like him.
Love him.
Love others.
And it all falls into place.

Heaven is ours—right now and forever.
A beautiful, wonderful gift from God
       through his Son, Jesus Christ.

My Lord's Prayer

This, then, is how you should pray: "Our Father in heaven, hallowed be your name, your kingdom come, your will be done, on earth as it is in heaven. Give us today our daily bread. And forgive us our debts, as we also have forgiven our debtors. And lead us not into temptation, but deliver us from the evil one."

Matthew 6:9–13

My father in heaven,
I praise your holy name.

Bring your presence into every minute
    of my day.
May your will be my will as
    I live my days on earth.

Continue to provide all that I need
    and help me understand
    that all I need is what you provide.
Forgive me. Forgive me for the sins
    I can't seem to stop
    and the ones from what I fail to do.

Lead me and help me always
    to forgive others in the same way.

Please pull me back from all
>   temptation and keep the devil far away
>   so that I am focused only on you.

Please grant all this that I may
>   live in your peace and
>   glorify you forever.
Amen

My All in All

The Lord is gracious and compassionate, slow to anger and rich in love. My mouth will speak in praise of the Lord. Let every creature praise his holy name for ever and ever.

Psalm 145:8,21

My Father in heaven,
      Lord Jesus Christ,
            Holy Spirit,
You are my all in all,
      more than I can comprehend
      and you love me.
Thank you.

You created the world.
      There is nothing beyond your power.
      You watch over all
      and you take care of me.
Thank you.

Your miracles are everywhere
      for believing eyes to see
      and you heal me.
Thank you.

You became human.
      You lived among us.
      You served us then and now
      and you died to save us—even me.
Thank you.

May I always be in awe
of your power and majesty.
May I always be aware of your gifts
of grace, love, peace, and joy
and may I always be grateful.
May I always treasure the great honor
and gift of friendship you offer me.

Thank you.

My Shepherd

Praise be to the Lord, for he has heard my cry for mercy.
The Lord is my strength and my shield; my heart trusts in
him, and he helps me.

Psalm 28:6–7

The Lord is my Shepherd,
   what more could I want?

He tends to me like one of his own
      because I AM one of his own
      sometimes lost,
      always found.

He is with me always
      loving,
      guiding,
      providing,
      protecting,
      saving.

He pours his blessings upon my life
      over and over.
My cup is full.

Thank you, Jesus.

He Died for Me

Then Jesus went with his disciples to a place called Gethsemane, and he said to them, "Sit here while I go over there and pray." He took Peter and the two sons of Zebedee along with him, and he began to be sorrowful and troubled. Then he said to them, "My soul is overwhelmed with sorrow to the point of death. Stay here and keep watch with me." Going a little farther, he fell with his face to the ground and prayed, "My Father, if it is possible, may this cup be taken from me. Yet not as I will, but as you will."

Matthew 26:36–39

GOOD FRIDAY

I can't imagine what Jesus went through -
        the sadness of being betrayed, denied
                by his friends;
        the pain of separation from his father;
the burden of bearing our sins on the cross;
the pain of his torn flesh from the lashes;
the sheer agony of dying by crucifixion.

All that—so long ago—for me, for you,
        to take away the stain of our sins.

How do we say, "Thank You"
        for so great a gift?

Bless My Reading

For everything that was written in the past was written to teach us, so that through the endurance taught in the Scriptures and the encouragement they provide we might have hope. May the God who gives endurance and encouragement give you the same attitude of mind toward each other that Christ Jesus had, so that with one mind and one voice you may glorify the God and Father of our Lord Jesus Christ.

—Romans 15:4–6

Lord Jesus Christ,

Bless my reading
      that I may understand your word
      and revel in your presence.

Bless my reading
      that I may not let my doubts overwhelm me.
Bless my reading
      that my faith becomes stronger with each day.
Bless my reading
      that I may know the joy of believing
      and thus the joy of life in Christ.

Lord Jesus Christ,
Bless my reading this day.

And as I read your word
    let me meet you with the faith
        of the Centurian;
    let me feel the comfort of your loving arms
        wrapped securely around me
        like a child;
    let me be immersed in the joy
        of your saving grace;
    open my eyes like the blind man;
    make me grateful like the leper.

Lord Jesus Christ,
Bless my reading this day.

Thank you.

   Joretta K. Klepfer

Thank You

In him was life, and that life was the light of all mankind. The light shines in the darkness, and the darkness has not overcome it.

John1:4–5

Lord Jesus Christ,
>   you fill me with joy.
Thank you.

You died for me;
>   you live for me.
Thank you.

Guide my life to reflect your love,
>   to live for you.
Thank you.

Just Pray

And pray in the Spirit on all occasions with all kinds of prayers and requests. With this in mind, be alert and always keep on praying for all the Lord's people. Pray also for me, that whenever I speak, words may be given me so that I will fearlessly make known the mystery of the gospel, for which I am an ambassador in chains. Pray that I may declare it fearlessly, as I should.

Ephesians 6:18–20

Just Pray!

Pray what's on your heart.
God will listen.
He's always waiting to hear from you.

Whatever your situation,
wherever you are,
there is no time that God does not want
your thoughts,
your joys,
your concerns,
even your questions.
Have you been called to the bedside of a
sick friend or family member?

Pray on your way.
Pray with the person who is ill.
The Holy Spirit will surround you
and guide you to do or say what is needed.

Have you just been told that you have a
        promotion to a better job
        or that the love of your life wants
            to marry you?
Pray and share your joy with Jesus.
Have you lost your job?
Pray your concerns and ask for strength
        to face the days ahead.

Did you just mail your resume?
Pray for God's will to be done.
Just pray!

Use whatever style suits you best.
God dictates no specific form,
        no specific place,
        no specific time.
Find what makes you comfortable
        and tune in to hear God's word for you.

Yes, that means listening.
You shouldn't do all the talking.
Your relationship is a two-way street
        so your conversation should be too.

What works best for me is deliberate
        quiet time in the morning
        before the day crowds in
        and then a constant vigilance
        throughout the day for times
        to pray and times to listen.

God speaks to us though his word,
    other people,
    nature,
    chaos
    and all circumstances.
We just need to be open to
    the conversation.

May you be blessed by your time in prayer
    whenever,
    wherever,
    however long,
    however short,
    whatever form it takes.

Jesus is waiting to hear from you.

Whatever Your Past

Whatever your past,
      let Jesus Christ be your future.

Open your heart to Jesus
He will open your life
      to love and laughter,
      to joy and peace.
He will guide you through
      each challenge,
      each heartbreak.

He's ready to welcome you with open arms.
Let him be your refuge.
Let him be your hope.
Let him be your friend.
Let him be your salvation.
Let him be your guiding light.
Let him be your companion and comforter.

Let him show you the way to live.

My Prayer for You

I pray that out of his glorious riches he may strengthen you with power through his Spirit in your inner being, so that Christ may dwell in your hearts through faith. And I pray that you, being rooted and established in love, may have power, together with all the Lord's holy people, to grasp how wide and long and high and deep is the love of Christ, and to know this love that surpasses knowledge—that you may be filled to the measure of all the fullness of God.

Now to him who is able to do immeasurably more than all we ask or imagine, according to his power that is at work within us, to him be glory in the church and in Christ Jesus throughout all generations, for ever and ever! Amen.

Ephesians 3:16–21

Author Biographical Information

Joretta Klepfer describes herself as an artist by choice, a writer/poet by chance, and a Christian by the grace of God. She and her husband, Bob, have been married for 51 years, have one son, Bob III, and live in Greensboro, North Carolina.

Joretta has a BA degree in mathematics from the University of North Carolina at Greensboro. Her varied career paths include four and one half years serving as Director of Christian Education and Youth Ministry at First Lutheran Church in Greensboro, North Carolina.

Her volunteer experience at First Lutheran extends over 48 years, predominately teaching and working with teenagers and also serving in many other areas, such as Church Council, Stewardship, Property and Worship Committees. She has also served in statewide ministry positions with the North Carolina Synod, ELCA.

In addition, Joretta is a self-taught artist specializing in hand-painted note cards.

Made in the USA
Lexington, KY
22 August 2016